Imprints

Imprints

Tracing Todays Behavior to Past Events

Fredrick D. Richardson

ISBN : 1-4196-2154-8

To order additional copies, please contact us.
BookSurge, LLC
www.booksurge.com
1-866-308-6235
orders@booksurge.com

Imprints

TABLE OF CONTENT

1.	Tracing The Raised Finger	1
2.	The Origin Of Ebonics	5
3.	What's In A Name	9
4.	Presence Of Conch Shells Have Meaning	15
5.	New Year And Watch Night	23
6.	The Origin Of Negative Behavior	31
7.	Music And Drums	37
8.	Being Smart And Proper	41
9.	Lining Hymns In The Baptist Church	47
10.	Negro Spirituals And The Blues13.	51
11.	Graveyards And Cemeteries15.	59

INTRODUCTION

The future of African Americans is directly connected to their past. Little that they know, each of them has a profound correlation to the other. As they march into the future, they must never forget the trails that link them to our past, however dim or glorious. Nothing happens by chance. There is a reason for everything. Those wise enough to investigate every unique behavior will find the true cause for such behavior. Many behaviors displayed today by African Americans can be traced back to a specific past event: Events of the past that left an indelible mark on their conscious, which drives their behavior today. Most have not the faintest knowledge as to what past events it were that guide their present behavior.

African descendants in North and South America had one special event that established their identity apart from other groups: Slavery. Because of the institution of slavery, many other smaller events became a spin-off from this institution. However, without the institution of slavery, African Americans would go largely unnoticed, and would have long become just persons whose skin may or may not have pigmentation or coloration. Slavery, not skin color, separated African descendants into a unique people who came up out of hard trials and tribulations, and eventually took their rightful place as major contributors, not only in the United States, but also in the world. And although severely damaged by inflicted institutional behavior, such behavior didn't stop this people from rising to heights unattained by those groups who remained free. Members of this group went on to invent the air conditioner, the washing machine, the clothes dryer, the elevation, the traffic light, the fountain pen, the helicopter, the lawn mower, the automatic sprinkler, corn flakes, instant coffee, and you get the point. God has placed in each individual the ability to rise above and beyond any present circumstance, no matter how grim. This group of African American shattered any false notion of inferiority, heaped upon them from many fronts, even the U.S. Supreme Court, in the *Dred Scott Decision of 1859,* where the Chief Justice, Roger B. Tanney, issued the decision. In that decision he asserted that the Negro has been regarded as a being of an inferior order for centuries. And that he had made absolutely no contributions to society. And, for his own good, this Negro must be kept in slavery. Furthermore, he stated, this Negro has no rights that a white man was bound to respect.

To my knowledge, no one has retracted or declared this statement to be false. Society pressed on, as if Tanney wrote the absolute truth. All too many white people and black people believed Justice Tanney's statement on inferiority, without appreciable evidence. This and the black man having been reduced to slavery, many had no other choice. Today, even after having dispelled Tanney's assertion and soared to heights unequaled, many still hold African Americans in disdain and scorn. The scars of slavery still remain. But many, whose ancestors never experienced slavery, became scarred as well. Slavery left no one untouched.

For certain, members of this targeted group (African Americans) today serve as a stark reminder that they are the off-spring of ancestors who, somehow, managed to survive the institution of slavery: But not without a high price and many, many, residual emotional and psychological scars. In fact, America herself was left scarred by the institution of slavery. I will issue some challenges for you to use to judge yourself. Thus, we have a paradox: Persons who instituted many of the brutal acts and conditions of slavery were themselves left damaged also, by the same institution.

Take the test and see if you were damaged from the institution of slavery. I challenge any of you among majority members of society, sometimes called "white," to name three persons, you personally know, with the first name MOSES. I will give you Moses in the Bible. The answer is likely that you do not personally know three persons with the first name Moses. Why not Moses? After all, he was the most prolific, dynamic, and heroic personality in the whole Old Testament of the *Holy Bible*. It was Moses that stood face to face with the Pharaoh of Egypt, who in his day was the most powerful king of the world, and told him God said "Let my people go." It was Moses who lifted a single rod and parted the vicious Red Sea. It was Moses that God kept on Mount Sinai for forty (40) days and gave Moses the Ten Commandments, written with the finger of God. It was Moses who prayed and God rained manner from heaven. It was Moses who struck a rock and water ran down from the rock, as it would have from a living fountain. It was Moses who was chosen by God to lead his children from 400 years of slavery in Africa, the city state of Egypt, to the promised land of Canaan. It was Moses who lifted a serpent on a stick, in the wilderness, and all who looked upon the serpent were healed from a sickness whose destiny was death. What a powerful man of God. And you mean you don't know three persons personally, with the first name Moses?

Why has a man of the stature of Moses gone miffed, silent, and ignored, in terms of his name being used today? After all, you can find plenty of people with the first names of other minor *Bible* characters such as Peter, James, John and even Judas (he sold Jesus for 30 pieces of silver). What traumatic event occurred which was so overwhelming that the name Moses became obliterated or eliminated from our culture? Under normal circumstances the name Moses would stand tall among us. It has silently been erased. I'll tell you what it was that blotted out the name Moses from among us. During the dark days of slavery, many slaves escaped to the north where they found freedom. Persons, such as Harriett Tubman, who herself was an escaped slave, wanted in every state, but came back many times to help slaves escape. She was so heroic and successful that millions of dollars were placed in bounty for her capture, dead or alive. She kept going back and rescuing slaves, but was never captured.

Slave owners took extreme measures to ensure that their slaves did not escape through the Underground Railroad, where Tubman and others were waiting to lead them to freedom. Harriett Tubman was dubbed as "Black Moses" because of the number she led to freedom. Her name became synonymous with Moses of the *Bible*, who led his people to freedom. When word would reach the slave quarters that Harriett was coming, slaves would sang out the old Negro Spiritual code song, "Go Down Moses, Tell O Pharaoh, To Let My People Go." Eventually, slave masters broke the code and took swift action. The cry went out from slave owners, over plantations and fields, where slaves worked, that anyone caught using the name "Moses" would befall much harm, including death. So the name "Moses" became virtually extinct, not only among the targeted group, but also among whites as well. We all act out behaviors shaped by events of the past. The problem is many are not aware of the rudiments of such behavior. The name Moses is but one example among many that guides our behavior today. This includes everybody. Our past guides our future behavior. This small book will share with you other instances where many specific past events are guiding our behavior today.

Such behavior, in reacting to events long past, is not limited to blacks. Whites are equally subjected to the same behavior. For instance, during the dark days of the Civil War, General William Tecumseh Sherman, named commander general of the Union forces, led Union troops throughout the south, burning down cities found in his path, including the city of Atlanta, Georgia. Many southerners saw much of their wealth evaporate before their eyes and go up in smoke. Therefore, General William T. Sherman became a hated man throughout the south. Today, you will be hard pressed to find a southern white man with the first name Sherman. In fact, you will hardly find a white man living in the north with the name Sherman. Blacks hardly ever use that name. You now know the event that placed the name Sherman in disdain. You can now judge the behavior, including your own.

Parents don't call their children together and teach them not to use the name Sherman. It is inbreeded, through socialization and acted out on the stage of life. Without a spoken word, certain action triggers certain behavior, and this behavior can now be understood.

It is virtually impossible, if not improbable, for any person to have been traumatized (made to suffer great emotional shock) by any event, let alone slavery, and come out of such an experience without any emotional scars. An event, as simple as a burglary, can force a homeowner to install burglary bars, purchase vicious dogs, purchase deadly firearms, install a burglary alarm system, install motion detectors, install motion sensor outdoor lighting, and completely fence their property in. Those burglary bars and other measures represent an emotional scar left behind from a specific act, a burglary, which has long past. We see that a simple event can trigger pronounced prolonged behavior.

During an experiment conducted by a national known company, over several years, dogs were used to determine if a single traumatic event could alter the their normal behavior. Dogs were set free in a large pin to roam at will. However, there were two separate feeding stations in the pin: One, stocked with leftover bones from fresh cut meat. And the other feeding station was stocked with daily fresh cuts of meat. The feeding station with the fresh cuts of meat was deliberately rigged with a low level charge of harmless electricity. At first, when the dogs were turned loose, they all went to the feeding station with the fresh cuts of meat. Later, the low electric charge was turned on so as to not harm them, but make them mighty uncomfortable. They all could feel an uncomfortable tingle from the charge.

Not long after this low level of electricity charge was felt by all the dogs, they immediately ran away from that feeding station and started to feed at the station with no electricity. That was the station that had bones only. Although both stations were bated with fresh bones and meat daily, after the low level electrical shock, all dogs only ate at the station baited with bones, where no electric charge was present. Even after the electricity was turned off at the station with fresh cuts of meat, they didn't come back. The dogs never returned to the station where they were initially shocked because of one single event. That fact alone does not tell the whole story. Many of the female dogs had puppies later on, and their puppies never visited the station with the fresh cuts of meat either. Somehow that experience, suffered as a result of the low level electrical shock, was transferred through socialization, to the next, and next, and next generation of dogs. Human behavior is no different from those of the puppies.

Like the puppies, humans today are reacting to events that occurred hundreds of years before they were ever born, and are left without a clue as to what initially triggered their behavior. Recently my laptop computer locked down, because a virus had invaded the operating system. This virus crept in, attached to a file, unbeknown to me. One thing for sure, this virus took control over the system that operated my computer. The human mind, like a computer, can be subtly invaded and imprinted with information unknown to the person whose mind it invaded. When this occurs, persons imprinted will be unconsciously guided into action, without the faintest clue as to what has caused them to act. This fact you will see more clearly as we move forward together.

This small book recognizes the fact that many formidable imprints were left on the conscious of African descendants in North and South America, more so than others. Many of these imprints can be traced directly to traumatic events related to a past experience that resulted in a traceable, identifiable behavior, displayed by many, even today.

When you are finished with this book, hopefully you will be able to identify many of the events and the behavior which drives and directly affect the action of many, especially African Americans, even today.

My purpose for writing this book, however, was to provide a greater understanding, a greater insight and a greater appreciation, for those who make up members of this targeted group (with a remote African ancestry). And, to show how many past events have resulted in pronounced behavior that has shaped, not only the lives of members of this targeted group, but also the lives of all who came in contact with them.

I bothered to list certain traumatic events and the association behavior, less we all forget and lose the sight of major identifying characteristics among us that make us who we are and serve as a direct link to past generations

Please read first, before you make a value judgment on the merit of this work. You may learn something. Who knows, you too may be in for a rude awakening in finding a connection to certain identified behaviors prevalent among yourself that can link you to past ancestors. Peace.

Fredrick Douglas Richardson, Jr.,

Great Grandson of slaved ancestors

PREFACE

EVENTS AND BEHAVIOR

A ll information contain below will identify a specific event in past history, particularly affecting African descendants in North and South America. You will also find how a display of specific behavior today, among the group already identified, is traceable to many specific events of the past. What is concluded from this survey is that our past history surely shapes our future actions, on a daily basis, although such predisposed behavior is unconsciously acted out. However, after reading many events described below, one should be able to trace many of today's behaviors to specific events of the past, heretofore unknown, thus connecting us with our past ancestors. We all are who we are, based on the sum total of all our life experiences. And without any one of those experiences (good or bad), we would not quite be who we are today. Our future is shaped by our past. None of us are immune from the action of others. We all have been affected by the action of others. We shall see to what extent as you read on. Stop if you must. Go on if you wish to know.

PROLOGUE

In America, the issue of race has permeated and infected members of society. It has been imprinted in the mind and conscious of citizens, leaving behind permanent scars and abject behavior. Too many have been hurt for too long, by way of racial categorization. We can do better America. This is a burden we must lay down. My book, *IMPRINTS,* challenges each American President and indeed every American citizen, to bring to an end the dividing of our citizens into racial categories. The fact to the matter is, there is only one race among mankind, the human race. This nation designed false racial categories, so as to imply that some citizens are more valuable than others. America is the freest nation in the world. Yet, we are the only nation left who categorizes citizens according to race. We have allowed, for too long, our citizens to be shackled and denigrated, by using visible identifiable physical characteristics, to determine a person's race. We know as a fact, that if a being can stand and walk upright, can laugh, cry, think, reason and plan, such a being qualifies as a human, which automatically makes him a member of the human race. From that point we are individuals, each with our own separate abilities, completely disassociated from our skin color.

There are ethnic differences among humans, because we don't all share the same history, language, culture, religion, morals, and beliefs. Assimilation will eliminate those differences. Rest assuredly that the differences in skin color and body features, among humans, are purely incidental to who they are and what they can achieve. Race, as a category, subdivides humans in terms of how they expect to be treated.

Race has become imprinted on our conscious and has haunted this nation for centuries. It must now come to an end. We can do it America. And we will do better, for the sake of our own human dignity and for the peace and tranquility it will provide our citizens for generations to come.

Mr. President, lead us out of this dreary, miry and dismal past of racial divide. Take us up and beyond every obstacle devised to abort the success of our fellowman. Put race in its place and leave it there: On the exercise track, where we run for fun. And when this divisive issue of race becomes oblivious, null and void, then we all can do as the rose, which was snatched up from the rose garden and thrown by the side of the road: Bloom where you are!!!! God, bless America.

Fredrick D. Richardson, Jr.

EVENT NUMBER 1

TRACING THE RAISED FINGER

EVENT: African descendants dismissing themselves from the presence of a group, especially in a church setting, with one finger raised in the air, and, with the head bowed as in a gesture of humbleness.

BEHAVIOR: Behavior described in the event above is traceable directly back to the dark days of slavery, when slaves needed permission to leave from the presence of their masters or overseers. To walk away from the presence of the overseer and not gain permission would have dying consequences. Such behavior would leave the overseer to conclude that the slave had become a runaway. Much harm would befall a runaway slave, if caught. To avoid this possibility, a code, consisting of the raising of one's finger high in the air, was developed and instituted throughout all slave quarters and states. It became a universal code throughout the south. This code is still practiced today, unknowingly, by many of the offspring's of former slaves. Most don't have even a clue. It goes back to the fields of their ancestors.

In the fields, slaves often had a need to relieve themselves of human excretion, while hard at work. If slaves needed to urinate (commonly referred to as "pee pee"), all they needed to do to gain the attention of their overseer, was to raise one finger in the air, high above their head, and drop their head. The bowed head represented humility, humbleness and extreme respect for authority, in the persons of the master and his overseer. The slave's raised finger also signaled the master or to his overseer that the slave's leave of absence would be short. It told those in authority the slave would return quickly to the toils of the field. The master or overseer would signal an answer by shaking his head up and down if the request was granted: Or, shaking his head from side to side, if the request was not granted. The raised finger became apart of the slave code system that conveyed a deeper meaning they all understood.

Two raised fingers had an altogether different meaning. Often time slaves needed to be excused for an extended period of time, for the same kind of body relief. For instance, if a slave needed to have a bowel movement (commonly referred to as "doo doo"), one finger would not suffice. In that instance the slave would need to raise up two fingers, high above his head, with his head bowed low and his back humped over, in a gesture of humbleness. Throughout this signaling process, the slave could not look his master or overseer in the eyes. That is why his head was bowed and his shoulders drooped over. He took this position prior to raising his finger or two fingers so as to not seem contentious or suspicious. Recognition of the two fingers by the overseer was crucial in the life of a slave. With such recognition a slave would have clear authority to be excused for an extended period of time to meet the needs as requested by his body.

Today we see people from this targeted group still signaling with a raised arm and finger, with bowed head and back slumped over. It is as though there is still a need for permission to be dismissed from the larger group. This behavior is merely a carryover from the past. Such behavior is carried out today, especially at official meetings and religious services. It is more prevalent among older members of this targeted group. Although the event that triggered or facilitated the need for members of this group to raise their finger and bow their head ended in the year 1865, the initial event was so pronounced and traumatic that members of this group still carry this tradition on, as if the master or his overseer was present at their meetings (remember the dogs that were shocked with a low level electric charge). Those raised in the south are more prone to raise the finger when leaving a meeting. Those raised in a southern rural setting honor this tradition above all others. However, even those who are members of the targeted group who migrate to other parts of the nation can be seen raising the finger when leaving meetings, also. Many have no clue as to what event it was that triggered this behavior.

Just like dogs continued to avoid the feeding station where a low level of voltage was located when they were initially shocked, now we see how human trauma becomes a driving force that shapes our behavior for generations to come. Behavior precipitated by extreme trauma becomes transmissible through mores, customs and traditions. What do we say today for certain behavior displayed because of some event of the past? To say we find out the rudiment cause of such behavior and learn from it. I say we reconcile our behavior through knowledge of the event it was that gave rise to the initial behavior. I say we make sure the past traumatic event that gave rise to today's behavior becomes null and void in the future. I say the more we know of the past, the better off we will be in the future. No, the raised finger is not a necessity today. But at least from it, we all can be thankful and appreciate the distance we have traveled from the initial traumatic event that gave rise to the raised finger in the first place. However, we may never know how far we have traveled from the slave fields of the south until we recognize our special traits and behavior, peculiar only to members of this targeted group.

EVENT NUMBER 2

THE ORIGIN OF EBONICS

EVENT: When members of this targeted group were unloaded from the vessels that brought them from their native land of Africa, they spoke their native languages indigenous to the people of Africa. The English language was unknown to them. Southern states of the United States that embraced the institution of slavery quickly passed laws outlawing the educating of slaves. Laws were also passed forbidding the mixing of slaves with free people who spoke and taught the English language. Thus was the condition that gave rise to the birth of Ebonics. Such a legal paradox set the stage for a self-fulfilling prophecy regarding a deliberate misnomer or falsehood told of descendants of Africa. Plantation historians, text book authors, Supreme Court Judges, and the majority community as a whole, held the notion that African descendants had a natural innate inability to learn. It was self-fulfilling in that no schooling was allowed so slaves could learn. Even an unwise person could have accurately predicted the targeted class would be unable to learn when nothing is taught. It is one thing to make an outlandish prediction. It is another thing to put your plan in place to make your own prediction come true. It is like placing broken glass and strips of nails in the path of a car and predicts that the car would not make two blocks without having a flat tire. Such a prediction or prophecy then would be self-fulfilling, in that you put your own plan in place to make your own prediction come true.

BEHAVIOR: Speaking broken English, especially among the targeted group, is often referred to as EBONICS. What is the origin of ebonics? Since schooling, during the period of slavery, was forbidden and the ability of the targeted group to mix with those who spoke the language properly was also forbidden, members of the targeted class were extremely limited in opportunities to correctly learn the English language. Without the opportunity to properly learn the only language slaves were allowed to speak, the targeted group was challenged with the task of carving out their own language and dialect as a means of communicating. This language, today referred to as ebonics, was based on the tongues the targeted group spoke before leaving Africa, and sounds they heard other foreigners speak who enslaved them. Today, this hybrid crude rudiment of the English language is still spoken in many communities. Those with a greater exposure to the English language, in terms of opportunities that require mastery, often look upon those who regularly resort to ebonics, as displaying a measure of ignorance.

In South Carolina many African descendants still speak a broken English called Geechee. This term Geechee was derived from the group who transported African descendants from their native soil to South Carolina known as the Portuguese.

It is important to note that every other foreign group who came to America from foreign lands, speaking only their native tongue, took the absolute same route of African descendants. They all came and spoke a broken English, even after attending schools in America where the English language was taught them. These other foreigners who came to America also were allowed to mix freely with members of society who mastered the English language. Still these new Americans spoke a mixture of their own native language and English. Yet no other ethnic group was so castigated for the way they spoke as was this targeted group.

This hybrid English other foreigners spoke did not cause them to become stigmatized or castigated with a label of ignorance. After giving full consideration to the plight of African descendants in America, their isolation from the social, educational, political and economic mainstream of life in America, I take my hat off to this targeted group. In fact, this group of African descendants should be congratulated and extolled; not demeaned, for being perceptive, intelligent and resourceful enough to create a means of communicating without any formal training or help from those who mastered the English language.

One may truthfully say that since slavery ended in 1865, why are some members of the targeted group still speaking ebonics today? The answer lies in the fact that immediately after slavery a plan was devised and instituted to ensure African descendants of former slaves have a permanent place in the basement of this great society. In fact, black actors of the past had to demonstrate their ability to speak Ebonics, no matter how much education the actors had, in order to land a role in movies. It wasn't until the early 1920's, in many southern states, those blacks were afforded an opportunity to attend public schools. Even when schooling was offered, they were grossly inferior to schools whites attended. Blacks were denied the right to attend schools with whites for fear they would learn, not because they were deemed to be inferior. Those who made such assertion knew better. They hoped others would believe their lies. Many did.

In order to land a job, actors, in the past, from this targeted group, had to pretend to be stupid. Such a movie role was designed to send a clear and certain message to society that members of this targeted group were inferior to other members of society. It is apart of this same self fulfilling prophecy where you put your plan in place to make your own prediction come true.

It should be advocated that all students master the English language. We also must come to recognize that children come from various backgrounds and conditions and they should not be condemned merely on the basis of speech. While in the remote community of rural Alabama called Nymph, in an obscure village of small farmers, I spoke the language carved out by my ancestors who settled there after the end of the Civil War when freedom came. I had little contact with others outside of my village. Yet I was taught the correct way to speak, at school and at home. We were ridiculed if we spoke correctly. We were labeled as being proper. However, speaking with a dialect of English had nothing to do with intellect. Moddie Daniel Taylor left my rural community to live with his father, Herbert Taylor, in St. Louis, Missouri. He became one of the six most important scientists in the world. It was much of his work that led to the development of the atomic bomb. He was a member of a team of scientists who worked on the Manhattan Project. He was head of the science department at Howard University. Look him up on the internet. We overcame the dialect issue and took our place.

EVENT NUMBER 3

WHAT'S IN A NAME

EVENT: During the period of slavery, those in the target class who were confined to that institution had only first names. It was made clear in the <u>Dred Scott Decision</u> of 1857, by the United States Supreme Court, that slaves were merely property of persons who owned them. They had no rights except those allowed by their master, who was the person that owned them. Therefore, slaves had only first names. Having been legally reduced to property, a last name for slaves would have denoted humanity, ancestry and heritage, since a last name is traceable to a family.

Slavery ended with the close of the Civil (uncivil) War. So did the tradition of assigning members of the targeted group first names only. The process and method of acquiring a last name, by members of this targeted group, left a lasting mark on them that still exist today. With this in mind we will fine out what's in a name.

BEHAVIOR: Immediately after the end of slavery in April of 1865, over 4,000,000 newly freed persons of African origin had the distinction of becoming whole persons. As such, members of this targeted group were thereby elevated from the former position of being merely private property to that of a full fledge human being, with certain rights and privileges heretofore unknown.

States receive funding from the federal government based on the number of citizens living in a particular state.

To determine the number of citizens living in each state, the United States Constitution requires a census be taken every ten (10) years where every citizen is counted. When Slavery ended in 1865, those 4,000,000 newly freed persons of African origin could now be counted. The U.S. Census required persons to be listed by family, using the family's last names. Therefore, states required former slaves to go to the county courthouse and declare a last name. These new names were registered in the Probate Court. Former slaves, most without former education (and we know why), had a new task of selecting themselves a new name.

The legally mandated uneducated newly freed persons of African origin took a natural approach in selecting names for themselves, much like other groups who suffered great hardship. Most members of the targeted group selected names associated with the kind of work they performed as former slaves. For example, those who worked at the mill took a last name of MILLER. For those persons who worked in the building trade, many took on the last name of CARPENTER. If, as a slave, one worked mostly in the fields, he would likely take the last name of FIELDS. On the other hand, if a former slave was used to sewing and made clothing, he would most likely call himself TAYLOR. Those who worked in the kitchen used COOK as a last name.

Members of this targeted group took on names associated with colors, such as GREEN, BLACK, WHITE, and BROWN. So then, a person, who while in slavery was name James, would, after slavery ended, call himself James Brown, or James Black; or James White; or even James Green. Others of this targeted group would reach back and draw from some dramatic experience, such as one who was to force to walk a long distance. Such person would most likely call himself WALKER., as in Jesse Walker. Many for the first time, were able to own a house and took on the last name HOUSE, as in Ben House. If there were many hills to cross in seeking freedom, one would take on the last name HILL, such as Norman Hill. Those who drove mule teams took on DRIVER as their last name. Many fruits were used as last names, such as CHERRY, PEARS and SIMMONS. Those who hunted wild game for food took the name of HUNTER. Game was located in the woods and many took on the name of WOODS.

Nature played a major role in providing opportunities for selecting last names. Many in the targeted group lived near great bodies of water, such as a river. Therefore former slaves took on last names such as RIVERS and WATERS. Cotton pickers took the name of COTTON.

In instances where persons who owned slaves treated them with some degree of kindness, when such slaves were freed, many took on their former owner's last name. However, most took an altogether different last name from that of their former slave owner.

This practice where people who suffered greatly, took names for themselves after nature, vocation, colors, or animals, has been prevalent among other people that are not apart of this targeted group. For instance, Native Americans took on names of animals, such as Running Bear, Little Beaver, Rain Deer, Crazy Horse, and Big Eagle, to name a few. They also used nature by taking on names related to nature such as White Cloud, and Rain Water. As a people who suffered, Jews took on similar names, such as Goldsmith, Silverman, and Rich (all associated with wealth, gold and silver). Members of this targeted group were no different when the need came for them to select a last name.

It is crystal clear that today, the off spring among persons of African origin who are also members of this targeted group, still have last names traceable directly to the aftermath of slavery. What's in a name? Much can be gleaned from the history of a person just by knowing the last name. Just because the person wearing a name, similar to those who suffered, appears to be apart of another group, don't be fooled. Members of those with African ancestry come in all colors, religions, national origin and so on. Many, to avoid hardship, denied any kinship to their relatives of African origin, not knowing their names were a dead giveaway.

If you wish to determine where in any particular city Blacks live, look in the telephone book for persons with the last name WASHINGTON. You will be hard pressed, for whatever reason, to find a white person with the last WASHINGTON. There is something in a name.

African Americans were not the only group affected by slavery. Slavery took its tool on white Americans also. Take the name Sherman. You will be hard pressed to find a white person using that name, either in the south or in the north. Why? As it turned out, it was Major General William Tecumseh Sherman who marched Union Solders across the South, burning down whole cities on the way. General Sherman took Vicksburg on July 4, 1863 and moved on to Tennessee where he took Nashville and Knoxville. On May 5, 1864 General Sherman marched on Atlanta, Georgia. Unwilling to leave valuable men behind for the purpose of policing, he evacuated the city, allowing citizens to move north or south, and burned it to the ground. He marched across Georgia, North and South Carolina doing the same thing, capturing and burning. Therefore, the name Sherman became hated and scorned. To this day, whites in general, refuse to name their offspring Sherman.

The name Moses, as mentioned before, went the same way as did the name Sherman. Today you will be hard pressed to find a white American with the name Moses. So as to not flaunt the name in the face of whites, African Americans backed off the name Moses also. The name Moses represented freedom. As slaves, the word MOSES could only mean an opportunity to escape to the land of freedom. When using the name Moses in songs or speeches, it represented trouble for the slave masters. Slave holders, in a unanimous effort, mooted and deleted the name Moses from among African descendants. Their effort hold true, to a large degree, today.

THE DOZEN, an offensive term among blacks, has roots stretching back to slavery days. If one is said to have been put in The Dozens, one can assume a negative reference has been made of one's ancestors; a mother or maybe a father. Well, why has the term The Dozen, become offensive to blacks only, and not whites? Historians have it that during slavery, the auction center would be filled with slaves in the AM. By evening time however, only a few would remain, those sickly looking, and old. To rid themselves of their human commodity, slaves were often bunched up in lots of 12 (Dozen) and sold at a discount price. Slaves resented this method as it provided a greater likelihood of being sold and separated from family. Today, blacks still take offense to being put in The Dozen. The term still has a reference to the family.

EVENT NUMBER 4

PRESENCE OF OLD CONCH SHELLS HAVE A DEEP HIDDEN MEANING

EVENT: Conch is a member of the snail family. Snails are commonly present in the Atlantic Ocean and the Gulf of Mexico. However, the larger snails are called conchs and queen conchs are located in the Caribbean Sea ONLY. Countries like the Bahamas and Jamaica are plenteous in Queen Conchs. The Queen Conch has a large opening and inside the opening is dark pink, in most instances. The Queen conch is shaped like a cone, where the large opening of the hard shell (white or beige on the outside) runs in length for about 12 inches, to a sharp end. It is difficult to find a person of African origin, with roots in the Southern section of the United States, who either had a conch shell in their home or know of such shells. What is unknown to many is how this conch shell became so prevalent among just this targeted group. We know for sure their ancestors never went on a cruise ship to the Caribbean. The answer is forthcoming.

BEHAVIOR: During the dark days of slavery it was common for ships to leave Western Africa with a load of human cargo. Often ships would leave with an overload of slaves, in case some died from inhumane conditions. Many on the slave ship became sick and infirmed from the same inhumane conditions. By the time ships reached the Bahamas, their second leg of the triangular slave trade rout, the human cargo was unfit for the market and nor ready to be sold. It would have been a waste of time and money to try and sell slaves that were sick and poor.

Slave owners had to decide what to do about this fragile, unlikely to sell human cargo. Slaves needed to be fat and healthy in order to get the highest price. To fatten those slaves up for sale in the United States, Cuba and other parts of South America, they were fed pure conch, which was an excellent food source and all protein. After about two weeks of eating conch, slaves were in good health and ready for travel to markets in the United States, including Richmond, Virginia and Charleston, South Carolina, Selma, Alabama and Mobile, Alabama. At the slave auction the cargo would be sold to the highest bidder.

In many instances extra conch was put onboard the slave ships in route to the United States, to ensure their human cargo would remain fat, healthy and fit for sale. Slaves, in many instances, were wise enough to keep a conch shell for their proof of right of passage. It was their evidence that the slave plantation, where they were sold, was not their home. Slaves didn't know where they were being shipped to. Even their initial owners didn't know who would buy their slaves until they were purchased and the auction block had closed for the day. They would be sold to the highest bidder, who could have been from any state in the southern section of the United States. But wherever they ended up, they wanted to send a message, by way of the conch shell, that they had come here, by way of a place that grew conch in the shell they held, from their native homeland. In understanding that, it was a chance that someone would eventually find the actual place they came from, using their conch shell to aid the search in tracing the slave voyage backward to Africa.

One could speculate as to why those slaves didn't just tell their children where they came from instead of relying on a Conch Shell. Well, if you take into consideration they couldn't speak the language and were denied the opportunity to learn, they did the best they could to preserve a piece of evidence that one day would shed light on their voyage from their native land. The conch shell will take us back to a crucial point in the voyage from Africa.

Today, if you inquire of members of this targeted group

who have now or had relatives living or who lived in the south, they either saw a conch shell or they know about it. Almost every home, especially in the rural section of the south, had this conch shell. More often than not, the conch shell served as a door stop. The conch shell was universal among persons of African origin living in the south. The problem is, most who know about the conch shells don't know what they represent. I am sure ancestors of this targeted group had absolutely no knowledge that the water the conch shell came from is the only water in the world where they grow. Yet they preserved their conch shells so future generations could find the place they stopped on the way to America's slave market.

As a member of the City Council, in the City of Mobile, Alabama, we were asked to donate a tract of land to the Veterans Administration, to establish a cemetery for veterans. By resolution the Council donated Hartwell Field for this purpose. Hartwell Field was a former multipurpose ball field converted into a police training academy. Many horses, used to patrol in certain situations, are located on this property. Representatives from the Veterans Administration came to our city to conduct test on the soil at Hartwell Field to ensure suitability. The test revealed that there were over 3,000 graves under Hartwell Field. This site proved unfavorable for a burier ground for veterans.

The City of Mobile sent workers over to Hartwell Field to see exactly who were buried at the old football field. Workers dug up two graves. In one of the graves they found a conch shell and a piece of chain. The two graves were closed and workers returned with what they found. City department heads set out to find the meaning of the chain and conch shell. Finally, I was called and was asked about the meaning of the conch shell and the piece of chain found in one of the graves.

In less than 10 seconds, I knew the meaning of the conch shell and chain. First of all, the two relics were a sure indication that slaves were buried on the site at Hartwell Field. This ball park had been built on top of a burial site for slaves. Secondly, the conch shell represented a message to the living which was: "This is not my home." Thirdly, the piece of chain found in the unearthed grave represented this message: "I came here against my will."

These conch shells are still lying around homes all over the south. The problem is too many are unaware of the deep meaning of the conch shells. Surely it is time to retrieve these conch shells and highlight the deep meaning each of them hold. They document the fact your ancestor traveled along the triangle slave trade route. It documented that the queen conch came straight from the Bahamas or some place in the Caribbean, and it is highly likely your ancestors left Africa and were shipped straight to the Bahamas on the way to the auction block in America. The conch shell meant that former slaves who preserved it thought such shell was important. This conch shell to them symbolized a notable event. It served to preserve their memory of a life-altering event. It was their Rite of Passage. It captured and characterized their voyage into profound abyss. It denoted their traumatic change in status. For them, It marked their passage into a different world and way of life It served to highlight a life transforming journey. It captured a moment in history indescribable otherwise. This conch shell provided future generations a link that connects the past. We, the offspring's of such former slaves, must also preserve these commemorative conch shells with the same high esteem. They are a piece of the puzzle that unravels the question regarding the origin of our ancestors. With the conch shell, at least you know you had ancestors who were shipped from Africa, and who were apart of the triangular slave trade.

On November of 2000, I went on a mission to Havana, Cuba, representing the City of Mobile, Alabama. Mayor Michael C. Dow accompanied me on this mission. While in the City of Havana I had the esteemed pleasure of meeting with officials and citizens of that city. We attended the VII National Assembly of Mayors. Mayor Dow addressed this assembly.

An Afro-Cuban named Luis Alfonso Lescaille served as interrupter for Mayor Dow because he was affluent in English. Luis was 26 years of age. I ask him if his parents or grandparents had a conch shell in their home. He stated his grandparents had one. While in Havana I interviewed many other Afro-Cubans whose ancestors had the conch shell also in their homes. However, none that I interviewed had a clue as to the meaning of the conch shell. It became clear to me that Cuba was definitely a part of the triangular slave trade. Many, possibly a majority of Cubans living in the City of Havana are of African ancestry. Like African Americans, the conch shell among Afro-Cubans is intact and preserved, and neither knows not why they preserved the shell. Cuba is located in the Gulf of Mexico and as such has no queen conchs.

While attending the National League of Cities Winter Conference in Washington, DC, I met a waitress when eating at St. Gregory Hotel, where I was staying. Her name was Yahairie Velez and she was born in Puerto Rico. She remembers the Conch Shell of her ancestors. It was kept in the house, in a safe place. In fact, she had an abundance of history about her island. She was able to trace her family back to Africa. She said when the Spaniards came to the island it was called Boricua, meaning Black. It was changed to Puerto Rico, meaning "rich port." She didn't know exactly what the Conch Shell meant, but she realized it was important enough for her ancestors to preserve.

I am indeed thankful to a friend, Karen P. Burrows Pontius, who was born in Long Island, Bahamas. On one of her visits home she brought me a gift from her native land, a large queen conch shell. Her father had gone fishing in their local village of Long Island called Cartwrights. He caught some queen conchs. She kept one of the conch shells and brought it back to me as a gift, not knowing the actual significance of what she was doing. It was that incident that unlocked the truth for me and sent me reeling with excitement. I knew from that moment I could find out the meaning of the Conch Shell.

I knew of the large sea shell, but I never knew the name of such a shell, or that it came from a sea creature known as the queen conch. When I saw the shell Karen gave to me, it reminded me of the same kind of shell that was in my grandparents' home. It was used as a doorstop. In fact, most of the homes in my native community, called Nymphs, had a large queen conch shell, too. We often placed the hollow portion of that big shell to our ear to listen for the ocean roar. We knew to place it back in its place. We knew it was important. We didn't know why. I never saw it outside of the house. We knew better than to take it outside. My grandmother hoarded it as if it was extremely significant and a precious jewel.

After learning where the queen conch shell came from, I set out to find out how prevalent the shell was in other parts of the south. After interviewing hundreds of people, I was shocked to find that the conch shell was very common throughout the south. Also, people of this targeted group, throughout the nation, either had seen the conch shell back in the south or knew of it. My next move was to find the relationship between the conch shell and slavery, since this shell came with our ancestors who experienced the institution of slavery.

When I studied the history of slave routes to America, it became too clear to me as to the reason our ancestors kept the conch shell. It symbolized a particular moment in time and a place, on their way to a final unknown destination. The shell, I am sure, lent hope that their dreadful plight would be traceable to a distance place they once traveled. Since I now know that place to be somewhere in the Bahamas, I may, someday, be able to find their native homeland. I urge members of this targeted group to go now, with haste, and claim your family's conch shell, left behind for you by your ancestors.

Use the conch shell to tell your ancestor's story, as a people who survived that treacherous journey, from their native land of Africa, through the Bahamas and over to this new land called America. Use the shell to show how your ancestors kept it as their right of passage. Use the shell to show how the queen conch shell was kept by your ancestors, in hopes that some day, someone would use it to reconstruct their journey, from Africa, through the Bahamas, and over to the United States of America. Use it hopefully, to have scientist establish an actual date and time your ancestors crossed the oceans and seas, before landing in America. But above all, seize the opportunity to highlight this lost chapter in history, by placing the queen conch shell in a lofty high place in your home, so as to cause those who come near to it to ask you questions out of sheer wonder. This will give you the opportunity to tell your ancestor's story. And you can reserve for them their rightful place of honor and wisdom and courage, for surviving a voyage, laced with oblivion, and survived, against all odds.

EVENT NUMBER 5

NEW YEAR AND WATCH NIGHT

EVENT: Each year, at the dawning of the New Year, members of this targeted group, comprising of those whose ancestors survived the institution of slavery, gather in churches around the nation, for Watch Night Service. Celebrating Watch Night is an event that has always come on the eve of the New Year. At the stroke of midnight, on January first, each year, a New Year is ushered in, with the sounds of bells ringing and guns shooting. All too many are lost as to the deeper meaning of this event. However, Watch Night and shooting of guns at the dawn of the New Year have a meaning dating back to January 1, 1863. The meaning may be lost, but the behavior of members of this targeted group is as prevalent and widespread today as ever before. In fact it is so pronounced that majority members of communities the nation over fire their weapons too, at the stroke of midnight, to denote the beginning of a New Year, or so they say.

BEHAVIOR: Throughout the U.S., members of this targeted group, who are also children of those who survived the institution of slavery, gather in churches, on the eve of each New Year. Such gatherings they call Watch Night. They gather, in the form of prayer vigils, in churches, to give praises to God for all His goodness and mercy and blessings and favor, throughout the year and in the New Year to come. It least that is what you will hear them say today, if you were to questioned the meaning of Watch Night. The initial meaning of such gatherings have long become lost, probably because out of fear of retribution. The initial event that brought about the first Watch Night meetings was a promise made by President Abraham Lincoln that he would issue a Proclamation, making slaves free, in all such states that met certain of his conditions. Well, many disbelieved President Abraham Lincoln would not actually carry out his promise. The family of Lincoln's wife and Lincoln himself owned slaves. President Lincoln had many well-to-do friends who owned slaves also, sending a cloud of doubt over President Lincoln's promise.

The eve of the promised date for President Lincoln to sign his promised Emancipation Proclamation, was December 31, 1862. The Civil War was being fought on every front. The south was holding its ground. Meanwhile the great abolitionist, Frederick Douglass, had already met with President Abraham Lincoln to convince him to issue such a proclamation. President Lincoln needed all the help he could get in bringing the south back into the union. As The Civil War raged on, the south was moving in on many fronts under General Robert E. Lee.

Frederick Douglass was convinced and he shared the same with President Lincoln that the role slaves played in assisting the Confederate Army, gave the South an unnecessary edge. Slaves cooked food for the Confederate Army. They maintained their horses, supplied their ammunition, they repaired their torn uniforms, tended to their wounded and indeed, some even fought in their battles. Setting slaves free in the south, Douglass reasoned, would place the Confederate Army at a grave disadvantage and it surely would lessen the number of fighting solders available for battle. With slaves removed as support for the Confederate Army, their own soldiers would have to leave the battle field and perform duties once assigned to slaves. If this happened, Douglass reasoned, the Union would indeed have the edge.

Frederick Douglass made another vow to President Abraham Lincoln. Douglass promised that if the President issued the Emancipation Proclamation, he would also help organize several regiments of black solders, to fight with the Union.

Douglass indeed organized the 54th and 55th regiments, as he promised. By sending these black soldiers deep into southern states, Douglass reasoned, slaves would see them and would more quickly, willingly and eagerly, honor the Emancipation Proclamation, by coming north and joining the Watch Night Union Army. Douglass had two sons who joined from New York, Charles and Lewis. The stage was set. Lincoln not only promised Frederick Douglass he would issue the Emancipation Proclamation, he made a public statement announcing a date to issue the epochal document. The target date for this extraordinary announcement was set for January 1, 1863, at the stroke of midnight. Therefore December 31st, the night before Lincoln promised to issue the Emancipation Proclamation, became important to the targeted group of African Americans. December 31, 1862 was also New Year's Eve, as well as.

And so it was, that free citizens of African origin began to gather on the eve of the date Mr. Lincoln promised to issue his Emancipation Proclamation, December 31, 1862. They gathered in states without slaves; not to watch the old year out and the New Year in, as many claim today, but to watch and see if President Lincoln, in fact, would indeed issue and sign his promised Emancipation Proclamation. Hence, since December 31, 1862, the night before New Year's, has been called Watch Night. The Proclamation reads as follow:

The Emancipation Proclamation
January 1, 1863
A Transcription
By the President of the United States of America:
A Proclamation.

Whereas, on the twenty-second day of September, in the year of our Lord one thousand eight hundred and sixty-two, a proclamation was issued by the President of the United States, containing, among other things, the following, to wit:

"That on the first day of January, in the year of our Lord one thousand eight hundred and sixty-three, all persons held as slaves within any State or designated part of a State, the people whereof shall then be in rebellion against the United States, shall be then, thenceforward, and forever free; and the Executive Government of the United States, including the military and naval authority thereof, will recognize and maintain the freedom of such persons, and will do no act or acts to repress such persons, or any of them, in any efforts they may make for their actual freedom.

"That the Executive will, on the first day of January aforesaid, by proclamation, designate the States and parts of States, if any, in which the people thereof, respectively, shall then be in rebellion against the United States; and the fact that any State, or the people thereof, shall on that day be, in good faith, represented in the Congress of the United States by members chosen thereto at elections wherein a majority of the qualified voters of such State shall have participated, shall, in the absence of strong countervailing testimony, be deemed conclusive evidence that such State, and the people thereof, are not then in rebellion against the United States."

Now, therefore I, Abraham Lincoln, President of the United States, by virtue of the power in me vested as Commander-in-Chief, of the Army and Navy of the United States in time of actual armed rebellion against the authority and government of the United States, and as a fit and necessary war measure for suppressing said rebellion, do, on this first day of January, in the year of our Lord one thousand eight hundred and sixty-three, and in accordance with my purpose so to do publicly proclaimed for the full period of one hundred days, from the day first above mentioned, order and designate as the States and parts of States wherein the people thereof respectively, are this day in rebellion against the United States, the following, to wit:

Arkansas, Texas, Louisiana, (except the Parishes of St. Bernard, Plaquemines, Jefferson, St. John, St. Charles, St. James Ascension, Assumption, Terrebonne, Lafourche, St. Mary, St. Martin, and Orleans, including the City of New Orleans) Mississippi, Alabama, Florida, Georgia, South Carolina, North Carolina, and Virginia, (except the forty-eight counties designated as West Virginia, and also the counties of Berkley, Accomac, Northampton, Elizabeth City, York, Princess Ann, and Norfolk, including the cities of Norfolk and Portsmouth[)], and which excepted parts, are for the present, left precisely as if this proclamation were not issued.

And by virtue of the power, and for the purpose aforesaid, I do order and declare that all persons held as slaves within said designated States, and parts of States, are, and henceforward shall be free; and that the Executive government of the United States, including the military and naval authorities thereof, will recognize and maintain the freedom of said persons.

And I hereby enjoin upon the people so declared to be free to abstain from all violence, unless in necessary self-defense; and I recommend to them that, in all cases when allowed, they labor faithfully for reasonable wages.

And I further declare and make known, that such persons of suitable condition, will be received into the armed service of the United States to garrison forts, positions, stations, and other places, and to man vessels of all sorts in said service.

And upon this act, sincerely believed to be an act of justice, warranted by the Constitution, upon military necessity, I invoke the considerate judgment of mankind, and the gracious favor of Almighty God.

In witness whereof, I have hereunto set my hand and caused the seal of the United States to be affixed.

Done at the City of Washington, this first day of January, in the year of our Lord one thousand eight hundred and sixty three, and of the Independence of the United States of America the eighty-seventh.

By the President: ABRAHAM LINCOLN

WILLIAM H. SEWARD, Secretary of State.

Frederick Douglass gave us all a glimpse of how the first Watch Night unfolded, when he wrote:

[1]"On the side of doubt, it was said that Mr. Lincoln's kindly nature might cause him to relent at the last moment, that Mrs. Lincoln, coming from an old slaveholders family, would influence him to delay, and to give the slaveholders one other chance.

Every moment of waiting chilled our hopes, and strengthened our fears. A line of messengers was established between the telegraph office and the platform of Tremont Temple (Boston), and the time was occupied with brief speeches from Hon. Thomas Russell of Plymouth, Mass., Anna E. Dickinson (a lady of marvelous eloquence), Rev. Mr. Grimes J. Sella Martin, William Wells Brown, and myself. But speaking or listening to speeches was not the thing for which the people had come together. The time for argument was passed. It was not logic, but the trump of jubilee, which everybody wanted to hear.

"We were waiting and listening as for a bolt from the sky, which should rend the fetters of four million of slaves; we were WATCHING, as it were, by the dim light of the stars, for the dawn of a new day; we were longing for the answer to the agonizing prayers of centuries. Remembering those in bonds as bound with them, we wanted to join in the shout for freedom, and in the anthem of the redeemed.

Eight, nine, ten o'clock came and went, and still no word. A visible shadow seemed falling on the expecting throng, which the confident utterances of the speakers sought in vain to dispel. At last, when patience was well-nigh exhausted, and suspense was becoming agony, a man (I think it was Judge Russell) with hasty step advanced through the crowd, and with a face fairly illumined with the news he bore, exclaimed in tones that thrilled all hearts: 'It is coming! It is on the wires!!' The effect of this announcement was startling beyond description, and the scene was wild and grand. Joy and gladness exhausted all forms of expressions, from shouts of praise to sobs and tears. My old friend Rue, a colored preacher, a man of wonderful vocal power, expressed the heartfelt emotion of the hour, when he led all voices in the anthem, Sound the loud timbrel o'er Egypt's dark sea, Jehovah hath triumphed, his people are free."

The scene described above occurred in Boston on the eve of President Lincoln issuing the Emancipation Proclamation. However, churches and coffee shops around the nation, in free states, held similar gatherings. They watched and waited, until the word came regarding the action of President Abraham

Lincoln, that indeed he had signed and officially issued, as he promised, the Emancipation Proclamation, setting slaves free in most states of the south.

Today, many members of this targeted group, shoot their guns at the beginning of each January First, at the brink of each New Year, a practice, though highly dangerous, still is a reality. Other members of this targeted group gather in churches as was done at the initial Watch Night, for an ecumenical celebration. Shooting guns initially had nothing to do with shooting the old year out and the New Year in. Gun Shooting on January First has the same meaning as gun shootings and fireworks on July Fourth, the day this nation acquired its freedom from England, in 1776. The difference is January First marks the day President Abraham Lincoln issued the Emancipation Proclamation, proclaiming slaves free. Many members of the majority community have virtually no understanding of Watch Night. Many have not as much as heard of Watch Night. However, members of the majority community also shoot weapons to celebrate the New Year.

It is crystal clear that Watch Night is directly traceable back to an event of January 1, 1863, when President Abraham Lincoln actually issued his epochal and renowned Emancipation Proclamation. Upon actually announcing the Emancipation Proclamation, African descendants marked and denoted that moment of freedom by firing their weapons into the air, and praising God, and shouting, and crying, and dancing, and so on. Many forms of this initial traditional celebration have been lost except the shooting of guns and prayer vigils. This tradition is currently carried out at the beginning of each New Year. The true meaning of this historical moment is nearly lost because our ancestors were careful as to not openly flaunt or exhibit jubilant behavior they deemed unwelcome by their previous slave masters. Indeed, survival for our ancestors superseded any other celebratory agenda of their day. They left it for other generations to correct many of the evils inherited from the old system of slavery. Their survival would allow their offspring's to take their rightful place in this new world one day, and rise to greatness that once prevailed in their homeland they called Africa, where their ancient ancestors built pyramids, practice medicine, wrote prescriptions, crown kings, built universities, built cities, and passed laws, long before any other people of the world did the same. In fact, the Dark Ages of their continent came with the institution of slavery.

EVENT NUMBER 6

THE ORIGIN OF NEGATIVE BEHAVIOR

EVENT: Slavery has left deep scars stamped indelibly on the minds and conscious of the offspring of those who survived that institution. We have already established the fact that often times children of those previously traumatized will unconsciously display destructive behavior, not fully understanding the root of such behavior. It is a recognized fact that all too many African Americans harbor resentment, envy and sometimes even hatred toward each other, for no apparent reason. Yet when we examine the rudiment and origin of such negative behavior, we find a clear and calculative motive for such destructive behavior, planted purposefully nearly 300 years past.

The following excerpts, copied from a document of an authentic speech, given in 1712 by Willie Lynch of the West Indies, to a group of Virginia slave owners, that sets forth one instance of the original and effective cause of the idea of human inferiority and iron grip of slavery that continues to more intensely shackle the spirit and psyches of African Americans to this present day.

HOW TO CONTROL YOUR SLAVED
(THE WILLIE LYNCH SPEECH OF 1712)
Gentlemen:

I greet you on the bank of James River in the year of our Lord one thousand seven hundred and twelve. First, I shall thank you, the Gentlemen of the Colony of Virginia, for bringing me here to help you solve some of your problems with slaves. Your invitation reached me on my modest plantation in the West Indies where I have experimented with some of the newest and still the oldest methods for control of slaves. Ancient Rome would envy us if my program is implemented. As our boat sailed south of the James River, named for our illustrious King whose version of the Bible we cherish, I saw enough to know that your problem is not unique. While Rome used cords of wood as crosses for standing human bodies along its old highways, in great numbers, you are here using the tree and the rope on occasion.

I caught the whiff of a dead slave hanging from a tree a couple of miles back. You are not only losing stock by hangings, you are having uprisings, slaves are running away, your crops are sometimes left in the field too long for maximum profit. You suffer occasional fires, your animals are killed. Gentlemen, you know what your problems are; I don't need to elaborate. I am not here to enumerate your problems. I am here to introduce you to a method of solving them.

In my bag here, I have a fool proof method of controlling your black slaves. I will guarantee every one of you that if installed correctly, it will control slaves. My method is simple, any member of your family or any overseer can use it. I have outlined a number of differences among the slaves and take those differences and make them bigger. I USE FEAR, DISTRUST AND ENVY FOR CONTROL PURPOSES.

Those methods have worked on my modest plantation in the West Indies and it will work throughout the south. Take the simple list of difference and think about them. On top of my list is "age", but this is only because it starts with "A". The second is "color" or shade, there is intelligence, size, sex, size of plantation, status on plantation, attitude of owners, whether the slave lives in the village, on a hill, east, west, north, south, have fine or course hair, or tall or short. Now that you have a lot of differences, I shall give you an outline. But, before I do that I shall assure you that distrust is stronger that adulation, respect or admiration.

The black slave after receiving this indoctrination shall carry on and will become self-refueling and self-generating for hundreds of years, maybe thousands

Don't forget you must pitch the old blacks against the young blacks, and the young black males against the old black males. You must use dark skin slaves against light skinned slaves, and light skinned slaves against dark skinned slaves. You must use the females against the males, and the males against the females. You must also have your white servants and overseers distrust all blacks, but it is necessary that your slaves trust and depend on us. They must respect and trust only us.

Gentlemen, these kits are yours to control. Use them. Have your wives and your children use them. Never mind opportunity. My plan is guaranteed, and the good thing about this plan is that if used intensely, for one year, the slaves themselves will remain perpetually distrustful.

END OF WILLIE LYNCH SPEECH

BEHAVIOR: The Willie Lynch formula for keeping slaves and their offspring on a perpetual path of resentment and distrust for each other has proven to be true. It is certainly alive and working among this targeted group today. The same method of carefully selecting a body of disinformation and mistruths to teach slaves, as Willie Lynch did, for the purpose of keeping them under submission, will have to be untaught in the form of counseling. Blacks and whites need to be counseled for being misinformed on the comprehensive plight of blacks and their total contributions, in spite of seemingly gigantic odds. Willie Lynch formula became systemic and institutionalized in movies, literature, history, and indeed socialization. In fact, it became a way of life.

The Dred Scott Decision of 1857 helped to substantiate the Willie Lynch formula when Chief Justice of the United States Supreme Court, Roger B. Tanney, issued the landmark epochal opinion in that case, which stated that blacks had no rights a white man was bound to respect, and that the black man must be kept in slavery for his own good. In March of 1857, when Dred Scott lost the decision, seven out of nine Justices on the

United States Supreme Court declared no slave or descendant of a slave could be a U.S. citizen, or ever had been a U.S. citizen. As a non-citizen, the court stated, Scott had no rights and could not sue in a Federal Court and must remain a slave. Judge Tanney sent a strong message, not only to whites but to blacks also, regarding their helpless state of shamefulness. Surely this extremely important decision had a negative effect on how blacks were viewed by the general populace and on how they viewed themselves.

At the time of Dred Scott Decision, there were nearly 4 million slaves in America. The court's ruling affected the status of every enslaved and free African-American in the United States. The ruling served to turn back the clock concerning the rights of African-Americans, ignoring the fact that black men in five of the original States had been full voting citizens dating back to the Declaration of Independence in 1776. This Supreme Court decision ensured a permanent place for this targeted group at the basement of the greatest society in the world.

The Lynch formula has yet to disintegrate. It is with us even today. African Americans have to overcome the fear of being labeled "racist," when seeking to eradicate from their group the mistrust and resentment instilled nearly 300 years ago by Willie Lynch in 1712 and the Dred Scott Decision of 1857.

No one will, or should do for you, what you can do for yourself. Placing all Africans Americans on a level mental playing field and on a positive and wholesome future course, should be paramount, without fear of retribution. The Willie Lynch philosophy must end now, and so must acting as agents for overseers or slave masters, whose time has come and gone. The Willie Lynch formula is only perpetuated when no one changes it. Even the Bible tells us the truth will set you free. If we always do what we always did, we'll always get what we always had. The formula must change for the outcome to be different.

One will be in denial to not recognize that today's behavior of African Americans, especially toward each other, is most often too negative. I feel sure that there is a better understanding as to where at least some of this negativism originated. The question is; what will be done about it? The answer lies with this same targeted group, whose past has been incensed in years of negative indoctrination. This group must reconstruct their past and teach these truths in the home and through socialization, and education. It is not an easy task to eradicate vestiges of the past where acceptance has been widely sanctioned by society. The truth, in terms of facts, must first surface; not with a tone of resentment, but as a means of eradicating years of misinformation consciously devised to demean the specific group of descendants whose ancestors were slaves. There will be sure resistance to any truthful information that places the rich historical contributions of blacks on par with any group in America or the world over. The fact of the matter is this targeted group excelled in spite of being subjected to the cruelest form of brutality. Yet their record of accomplishments was kept obscured. Some already deem exposing the truth and denouncing lies told of this targeted group as a form of hatred. America will be free only when the truth is told and the past reconciled to the extent that all is validated in history. The mandate and necessity to make the truth known, of this targeted group, far outweighs any fear of denunciation for doing such.

I see a direct link to destructive behavior among children of this targeted group and their lack of knowledge as to who they are and from whence they come. Text book writers have consistently left out of the books the history and accomplishments of this targeted group. How can one feel good about one's self when he/she is convinced his ancestors have made no contributions toward the nation's wellbeing? When you can start from preschool and go all the way through college, and never have a text book written by an African American, such an experience will shape your mentality in a negative manner. Not only does it provide you with a negative view of yourself and ancestors, it also supports others in their negative view of you. Truth to the matter is African Americans have, under the most trying circumstances, soared far beyond others who were unrestricted in their quest to achieve. The task now is to force text book writers and historians to record the true achievements of this targeted group, in all categories, as well as all other ethnic groups. When this happens, you will began to see much of the negative behavior, seen among this targeted group, dissipate and fade away into oblivion and America will be stronger.

EVENT NUMBER 7

MUSIC AND DRUMS

EVENT: No music in the world can be compared with that of African Americans. Unlike other groups, their music is denoted and established by a very strong beat of drums: Not just some small drums, as used in other cultures, but large drums with a loud and pronounced beat. Clearly, music from this African American group was born out of hard trials and tribulations, and can now be recognized apart from all others, everywhere in the world. This feat was not a stroke of luck, but was a result of a unique experience, steeped deep down in southern slave plantations, as well as the mother Continent of Africa. America's rich diverse culture, that includes music, was derived from the melting of people indigenous to other nations, who came to this nation for various reason, including the perpetuation of the institution of slavery. Yet this mixture of people and cultures has made the United States of America the most sought after nation of the world. Many have placed themselves and their families in great perils trying to reach America illegally. Many, after reaching this country had to face other barriers such as understanding the language.

Languages of descendants of Africa were spoken in rhythmic tones. Therefore inhabitants of that region of the world used drums to communicate with each other. The drum could carry a message over a long distance because of its loudness. A raised or lowered bead carried a distinct meaning. Therefore when African slaves were sold in America the drum was disallowed immediately. Slave owners feared slaves beating drums. They feared drums would be used by slaves to so as to organize uprisings without their knowledge. Native Americans used smoke to communicate. They were able to communicate, from tribe to tribe, by way of smoke signals. drums were used among African descendants as was smoke among Native Americans, to send messages. It wasn't until surrender came that the drums were allowed again.

BEHAVIOR: African slaves were kept under close scrutiny for fear they would somehow escape and inflict harm among those at liberty. Many spoke varied and sundry languages. Those who spoke the same language were most often separated, for fear they would plot and scheme their way to freedom. The name of the game was to deny access to communicate with each other. Well, since the drum beat was a major form of communication, slave owners soon outlawed drum beatings. No one was allowed to beat the drum during slavery. However, slavery ended in April of 1865.

It was after slavery ended that African Americans were finally able to beat their drums. Although there are no appreciable records to indicate members among this group who sought to establish a communication link among each other, by way of the drum beat, the drum, after slavery ended, became a permanent fixture as a musical instrument. African Americans beat their drums today as if there is a sense of urgency, and as if the very drum beat itself has a special message just for them. This instrument became the very source of their musical rhythms.

Until the beat starts and is firmly established, when music is being played among African Americans, there is little or no body movement. But at the first beat of the drum you can notice body movement among this group. Jazz, Blues, Soul, Rock, even Spirituals, all have this mighty beat of the drum. It seemed this group had to make up for times their drums were forbidden. But in doing so with the drum, this group has established itself as pioneers in American music and surfaces to predominate, not only in America, but indeed around the world. Their music was played in Japan, China, Africa, France, Italy, Spain, Brazil,

Argentina, Mexico, Poland, Slovakia, Warsaw, and other nations I traveled to.

Many are of the notion that those of African descent are born with a natural tendency to dance, unlike those of Euro descent. I beg to differ. If you wish to bring African Americans to a screeching halt on the dance floor, put a Hank Williams' number in the CD player and watch them stop dancing. On the other hand, if you wish to see Anglo Americans rush to the dance floor, keep playing Hank Williams. The truth is, whites dance well when music of their ancestors is playing. The same is true of blacks. Each group can and will dance when the right music is played. For the targeted group, they listen for the drum beat first and since all can watch the make the various moves within the established beat, it would appear that their dance is natural. It was all learned around catering to the beat of the drum.

American Country Music is unique on its own. The beat in country music is established by the steel guitar, not the drum. Therefore, it is clearly separated from African American music. Anglo Americans and African Americans have many similarities in their music. The message in Blues and the message in country music are basically the same. The drum beat separates the two. From time to time you will notice a soft drum beat in country music. But that is the exception, not the rule. Anglo Americans didn't rush to beat the drum because of its origin. Slowly this practice of ignoring the drum is coming to a screeching halt.

Ignoring the drum is like ignoring GRITS, a popular breakfast food, mostly served in southern slave states. There is no big outcry about grits in the south. They are on the menus, but often you may have to ask if they are served. It is like grits bring shame on the institution or restaurant where they are being served. But go to every house in these southern states and you will most likely find grits. It is one of the most popular items among breakfast foods.

Well, African descendants taught Americans how to grind corn into grits. Therefore, only in mostly slave states can you find grits. Yet many northern and mid western states like

Nebraska (Nebraska University's symbol is CORN HUSKER), Kansas, Iowa, Michigan, Ohio, Wisconsin, Indiana and Illinois are states located in the corn belt; not Alabama, Mississippi, Louisiana or even Georgia (grits country). But you will be hard pressed to find grits located in states within the corn belt. Many citizens living in the Corn Belt states have never even heard of the word grits. So we find that grits are not so much related to where the corn is, but who were able to grind corn into grits. Therefore, drums and grits have something in common; African origin, southern heritage, ascription to descendants of slaves, and loved by those who bothered to understand the uniqueness of them both.

EVENT NUMBER 8

BEING SMART AND PROPER

EVENT: Among descendants of slaves it is not acceptable to either be smart or speak proper in all too many instances. My own son was attacked in his school's toilet, by fellow African American students, simply because he made an "A" in math. All too often, among African Americans, it is a putdown when someone is referred to as "SMART" or "proper." If the statement is made: "He thinks he is smart," such a statement is meant in a negative sense, among African Americans. One is not being complimented, although being SMART should be desirable, when labeled in such a fashion.

Being proper carries the same negative connotations as being SMART. When someone is said to be speaking correct diction or proper English, many among African Americans consider such correct diction as "BEING proper." Now "Being Proper" is not a compliment. It is a direct putdown. Consequently you find many very intelligent African Americans acting otherwise, just to eliminate the probability of being labeled. They speak broken English just to get along.

So, the issue before us is how did such negative behavior, such as condemning intellect, become prevalent among descendants of slaves, especially since education and knowledge is basic among all other groups. What happened to this group that caused them to fear being labeled as intelligent and having knowledge, openly? Like everything else, there is a reason for such behavior that can be traceable directly to a specific event, or a set of events. Only in knowing the root cause of this currently practiced negative behavior can an abatement process begin. The event that precipitated this negative behavior can be found in the paragraphs below.

BEHAVIOR: As has been discussed before, for several hundred years African descendants, in America as slaves, were forbidden any type of legal schooling. Any slave caught reading was subject to being publicly whipped with many stripes and could even be put to death. Such a violator could be subjected to many other painful acts of punishment. The point was made crystal clear by those in authority that slaves and their descendants were not to be educated. Anyone caught aiding and abetting this targeted group in reading or other forms of education could and would be subjected to the same harsh punishment as the slave himself.

When slavery ended in 1865, an effort was made by several philanthropic organizations, including the Quakers. The Dutch organized the Free Dutch Reform Schools for ex-slaves and their descendants. John D. Rockefeller established the Rockefeller Foundation, to assist ex-slaves and their descendants in acquiring an education. Perhaps the greatest single contributor toward the education of ex-slaves and their descendants was Julius T. Rosenwald. His Rosenwald Foundation provided teachers, supplies and schools, throughout the south, for the express purpose of educating blacks. Many teachers, early on, in these freedmen schools were white women. The first school I attended in the mid 1940's, in rural Conecuh County (Nymph Junior High School), in Nymph, Alabama, was initially a Rosenwald School. Today, Tuskegee University (in Alabama) is the repository for old documents on Rosenwald Schools in Alabama.

Southern states were slow in establishing public schools that educated blacks. Many states waited until the early 1930's before opening their doors to publicly educate blacks. Southern states made sure teachers, equipment, supplies, books and the schools themselves, assigned to blacks, were all substandard to those white students attended. The goal, from the start, was to eliminate blacks as competitors. However, the scars left by forcing blacks to fear education during slavery and its aftermath still exist today.

During slavery, fear fell on every house within the slave quarters, where a single inhabitant could read. Fear came because when the old slave masters found out that one of his slaves could read, not only was the reader in trouble, but the entire house, as well as those living in the slave quarters. Slave masters figured that if one could read he or she probably taught others. So all those living in the house where a reader lived were in constant fear and that fear permeated and flooded the mind of those living in shanties and huts throughout the slave quarters.

An educated or learned black person had to act uneducated, unlearned, illiterate, stupid, brainless, or dense, in the presence of a white person or a domestic servant (in-the-house black person). Every southern black person, through socialization, learned the lesson of staying in your place, pretending you didn't know what you knew. By 1958, when I finished high school in rural Alabama, I was denied the legal rights to attend the University of Alabama. Only whites could legally attend that university. In fact, I was denied the right to attend the high school in the county where I lived, Conecuh County. The educational system, owned by the state of Alabama, established a County Training School, only for members of this targeted group to attend. The reasoning was we were born innately inferior to white students who attended the high school. Therefore, a school was established to train me and others of this targeted group because, supposedly, we were unable to be educated, as supposedly our white counterparts were.

Today, with all of the changes we have witnessed in society, in every walk of life, it may be difficult for some to understand the reservation some blacks have in overtly or openly showing their high level of intellect. They see a need to keep the fact they are smart low keyed.

It is like not using the name MOSES. This behavior is somehow built in and ingrained. Many black kids are ridiculed when making high marks in school by members of their own group. They are often taunted as acting "white," as if only white students are suppose to be smart. Being "proper" in the black community is frowned on. Even to speak proper could bring shame on one, including among certain African Americans, especially in the south. Many of the disturbances in our schools are directly related to the fact that many African Africans prey on fellow students who excel. It is like a flashback to slavery, where being educated would bring harm to the entire slave quarters.

My mother was a pioneer school teacher, sent to Conecuh County, Alabama as her first assignment. She eventually married my father, Fred Richardson, Sr. They had an open account at the Sid Lambert General Store, in Evergreen, Alabama. When time came to pay their account up, my father had my mother, Helen, to refigure his bill. Sid Lambert had blacks bluffed into not challenging his figures, no matter how inflated. The fact was blacks feared the outcome if Sid Lambert had an idea they were smart. Well, my mother Helen challenged "Mr. Sid" arithmetic. He was asked to refigure as she had reached a different conclusion, in her favor. Sid Lambert became so infuriated with my mother and father that he banned them from shopping in his store, ever again. His fear was they would send a signal to others who may have found out that their bill may have been inflated also. The point is, education was feared, when it was attained by a member of this targeted group.

Until those in charge of the system take the time and consider the whole slavery experience and its aftermath, we will continue to miss the mark in determining the root cause of this dysfunctional behavior, that is adversely oppose to a quality education. Most, who are acting out their frustration toward those who are educated, have not the faintish knowledge, or the slightest idea, as to how and why they are acting the way they do. It will take a journey back into time and history for them to understand their own destructive behavior, and the rudiment cause thereof. Again, some will say you are teaching hate, if you take students back in time, for them to gain an understanding about themselves. However, there is no other choice that I see. This comprehensive education that includes rudiments of the past should be taught to all, not African Americans only.

EVENT NUMBER 9

LINING HYMNS IN THE BAPTIST CHURCH TRADITION

EVENT: If you would visit a Baptist Church where church goers are basically made of members of the targeted group, such as National Baptist, you will find a unique opening for the 11:00AM worship service. Deacons will gather in the front of the congregation. One will stand and line a Hymn. When he is finish with lining the Hymn, the whole congregation will chime in and sing the words just lined by the deacon. Midway through the Hymn, the deacon will motion for the congregation to stand. Nearing the end of the Hymn, he will motion for them to be seated. When they are seated, a deacon will drop to his knees and offer a prayer. This process is repeated over and over, until devotion service is over.

Well, in other churches, including Southern Baptists, you will not witness an open prayer (devotion) meeting just before the start of the 11:00AM worship service. Basically, you will hear opening words from the minister and the choir will sang a congregational song. The order of service described in the first paragraph is relegated to only the Baptist Church of the targeted group. Nothing happens by chance. There is a reason for deacons behaving in the manner described above. It is also noteworthy to say that this behavior in basically universal among this group. It is time to find out why and discover a piece of history that makes this group unique in who they are.

BEHAVIOR: We have established the fact that slaves

were denied the right to read or to be educated, legally. So, when churches were established in various communities, after slavery, there were only a very few to be found, ex-slaves, who could read. However, there were some. The few who could read would come to the front during church service, and line the Hymn for those who could not read. For instance, the one who came to the front would stand and line the Hymn, "A CHARGE TO KEEP I HAVE." The deacon who lined the hymn would stand and sound these words:

A charge to keep I have
A God to Glorify

The whole congregation would chime in by repeating after the deacon, "A charge to keep I have, A God to glorify." At that point the deacon would line out the second part of the verse to the song:

Who gave his son my soul to save
And fit it for the sky

The congregation would chime in again and repeat the finishing words to the first verse to this song. When this process is completed, the deacon will move on to the second verse and repeat the process by lining:

To serve this present age
My calling to fulfill

When the congregation finishes with repeating the words just lined by the deacon, it is time for the deacon to motion for them to stand while he gives the finishing lines to this Hymn:

O May in all my power engage
To do my master's will

When these words are repeated by the congregation, it is now time for the deacon to motion for them to be seated. When this is done, another deacon will bow on his knees and lower his head while offering a congregational prayer. When the prayer is finished another deacon could line another Hymn, depending on what time it is. If another Hymn is to be lined, the process will be duplicated, except a different deacon will line a different hymn. Another favorite Hymn would be:

The day is past and gone

The evening shades appear

When the deacon has finished lining these words, again the congregation will follow suite by repeating the same words in the form of a song. At the end of this process, the deacon will line the second part to this first verse:

O may we all remember well

The night of death draws near

These words, when lined, will complete the first verse. Usually, if time permits, the deacon will line a second verse:

We lay our garments by

Upon our beds we rest

The congregation will sing these words as lined by the deacon. Upon lining these words, the deacon will ask the congregation to stand again. It is now time for the deacon to finish lining the second verse:

So death will soon disrobe us all

Of what we here possess

At this point the deacon will ask the congregation to be seated again. Another deacon will bow on his knees and offer a congregational prayer. It is about time for service to start. When the deacons chime out a lively gospel song, the pastor and choir will file in and take their place in the pulpit and choir loft. The pastor is now in charge and the eleven o'clock worship service is ready to start, all over America.

The point to be made is the fact that deacons are still standing before the congregation, lining Hymns like they did when members of the congregation could not read and needed the Hymns lined in order for them to follow along. Today, most members of church congregations are educated. Yet deacons still stand before the congregation as though we were back in the time of slavery.

Many members of these congregations are largely unaware as to the reasons why their deacons stand before them and line Hymns, in what is commonly called Devotion Service. Many are unaware that this is a practice that was carried over from slavery, at a time when their ancestors were forbidden to read. They may be unaware that lining Hymns is another way for one to read for a congregation, who, at one time in history, were forbidden to read for themselves. There is certainly a connection between lining Hymns and slavery. It is when we all understand this connection that we can hold this practice in deep reverence for those who have gone before us, who figured out a way to praise God through songs, in spite trepidation and fear.

EVENT NUMBER 10

NEGRO SPIRITUALS AND THE BLUES

EVENT: Negro Spirituals, like the Blues, were born out of hard trials and tribulations, and heartaches and pains, and disappointments. There is definitely a correlation between Negro Spirituals and the Blues. They are sung in meters, short and repetitive. The roots to these songs can be traced to slave quarters and cotton fields throughout the south. They are both truly songs that impacted and influenced the music of America. Many of the Negro Spirituals parted from the Blues in that slaves added codes to the words of songs. When they sang, they often were sending messages to the larger group. If we listen today, we can very well find the message intended for the God they served, as well as all seeking to find the way to freedom.

BEHAVIOR: The Negro Spirituals were born in the time of slavery. The one identifying characteristic for Negro Spirituals is that they are short and repetitive, that is to say, they most often repeat themselves. Often time those Spirituals will have a hidden meaning that slaves can understand. A song as simple as "Come To Jesus" can easily be identified as a Negro Spiritual because of its repetitiveness. The song goes like this:

Come to Jesus, Come to Jesus
Come to Jesus just now.
Come to Jesus, Come to Jesus
Come to Jesus just now.
He will save you, He will save you

He will save you just now,
He will save you, He will save you
He will save you just now
He will save you, He will save you
He will save you just now
He will save you, He will save you
He will save you just now

In the National Baptist Church, during First Sunday 11:00AM Service, the choir will often lead a Negro Spiritual such as "I know It Was The Blood," which goes like this:

I know it was the blood
I know it was the blood
I know it was the blood for me,
One day when I was lost
He died upon the cross
I know it was the blood for me.
He hung His head and died
He hung His head and died
He hung His head and died for me,
One day when I was lost
He died upon the cross
I know it was the blood for me.
He's coming back again
He's coming back again
He is coming back again for me,
One day when I was lost
He died upon the cross
I know it was the blood for me.

There were other Negro Spirituals that were intended to send messages to the general slave population. Many of the songs were laced with codes. Take for instance the Negro Spiritual entitled "Deep River." What has happened is congress has passed the *Fugitive Slave Act* which now gives slave owners the legal authority to go north and catch and bring runaway slaves back. Prior to this if a slave made it to a state that didn't practice slavery, that slave would become free. This new *Fugitive Slave Act* made it more difficult for runaway slave to escape the master's dragnet.

Slaves were, after the Fugitive Slave Act, required to travel all the way to Niagara Falls, Canada, to be safe from the possibility of being captured. However, they would have to cross the swift and deep Niagara River. Many slave masters realized slaves were traveling to Canada, so they made a hideout near the most shadowy section of that river. However, in knowing this, slaves would have to travel to the deepest and most unlikely section of the river to cross. Many slaves couldn't even swim. In the song "Deep River," the lyrics pertaining to Deep River had to do with the deepest section of the Niagara River where slaves had to cross.

The reference to their home being "over Jordan," in the song, had nothing to do with a river the Children of Israel crossed, when led across the Jordan River by Joshua, into the Promised Land. That was the message they wanted their master to receive. "My home is over Jordan," had to do with crossing the Niagara River into Niagara, Canada. In the song they asked slaved the question: "O don't you want to go.... Where all is peace". Words to the song Deep River, is recorded below for your review.

Deep river,
My home is over Jordan.
Deep river, Lord,
I want to cross over into campground.
O don't you want to go
To that gospel feast,
That promised land
Where all is peace?
O don't you want to go
To that promised land,
That land where all is peace?
Deep river,
My home is over Jordan.
Deep river, Lord,

I want to cross over into campground.

There were other Negro Spirituals that contained messages for salves such as Swing Low Sweet Chariot. Again, this song had reference to someone coming to carry them home. They made it look as if a chariot would be let down from the sky to take them back to heaven. However, they had coded the song to signal when someone would be coming to take them to freedom.

SWING LOW SWEET CHARIOT

|: Swing low, sweet chariot,
Comin' for to carry me home!
I looked over Jordan and what did I see,
Comin' for to carry me home!
A band of angels comin' after me,
Comin' for to carry me home!
|: Swing low, sweet chariot,
Comin' for to carry me home!
If you get there before I do,
Comin' for to carry me home,
Jess tell my friends that I'm acomin' too,
Comin' for to carry me home.
|: Swing low, sweet chariot,
Comin' for to carry me home!
I'm sometimes up and sometimes down,
Comin' for to carry me home,
But still my soul feels heavenly bound
Comin' for to carry me home!

This song meets the criteria for a Negro Spiritual in that the verses are real short and they repeat themselves. Being short and repetitive had to do with the lack of education. Slave masters ruled out education for slaves from the outset. They knew education was power in itself. Slaves were to be powerless. Their only power was to come from their master.

Well, trouble arose when members of this targeted group created music that stirred the soul of those who heard it. It was called the Blues. Such songs were written about everyday life in the city and on the farm. Blues singer B. B. King, from Indianola,

Mississippi, has been referred to as "King of the Blues." Blues, like the Negro Spirituals, are short and repetitive. In a larger sense, they both sound alike. Many Christians deeply opposed the Blues because they accused the singer of taking music out of the church and taking it into Juke Joints across this nation.

The song below was recorded by B. B. King, Trouble, Trouble, Trouble:

TROUBLES, TROUBLES, TROUBLES (King, Ling)

Troubles, trouble, troubles, troubles is all in the world I see

Troubles, trouble, troubles, troubles is all in the world I see

Oh sometimes I wonder, wonder what is gonna become of me

When I wake up early in the mornin', blues and troubles all
    around my bed

Oh when I wake up early in the mornin', blues and troubles all
    around my bed

Oh I never will forget people, the last words I heard my baby
    said

She said I'm leavin' you in the mornin', BB and cryin' won't
    make me stay

She said I'm leavin' you in the mornin', BB and your cryin' won't
    make me stay

Ah the more you cry honey, the farther you're goin' to drive me
    away

Yes all right...(guitar solo)

Oh if you just got to go baby, I hope you will come back one
    day

Oh yes if you just got to go baby, please come on back some
    day

Oh but I never will forget baby, baby the way we used to love
    and play

As you can see, the song Trouble, Trouble, Trouble meets the criteria for a Negro Spiritual and a Blues. Verses are repetitive and as such caused a stir in the churches. In fact when I was a child I was not allowed to turn the radio to Randy, in Gallatin, Tennessee, who often played the Blues. My Grandmother Maggie resented the Blues. Therefore I had to find another station, until she went to sleep. B .B. King wrote another song classified as the Blues: Woke Up This Morning.

WOKE UP THIS MORNING (MY BABY'S GONE) (King, Taub)

I woke up this morning, my baby was gone
Woke up this morning, my baby was gone
I've been so bad, I'm all alone
I ain't got nobody stayin' home with me
I ain't got nobody stayin' home with me
My baby she's gone, I'm in misery
Well baby, I'm all alone
Yes baby, I'm all alone
I ain't had no lovin'
Since my baby's been gone
All right...(guitar solo)
Oh baby, I'm all alone
Oh baby, I'm all alone
My baby she's gone, I'm in misery
Oh baby, come on stay with me
Yes baby, come on stay with me
My baby she's gone, I'm in misery
Oh baby I'm all alone
Oh baby I'm all alone
I ain't had no lovin' since my baby been gone

By now you should be able to see the resemblance between the Blues and Negro Spirituals and have some understanding as to why it took B. B. King and others years before they received proper recognition. It took Elvis Presley and others, who capitalized on songs long written by Blues singers, before the Blues took its rightful place. Take a look at a song written by Blues Singer, Howling Wolf and see if you can see why it is called the Blues: The Going To Mordor Blues:

THE GOIN' TO MORDOR BLUES
(Lyrics by Howling Wolf)

Well I'm goin down to Mordor,
'Cause the Master told me so,

Well I'm goin down to Mordor,
'Cause the Master told me so.
Yes I'm a-goin' to get my ring back,
I gotta pick up my feet and go.
Well it was taken by the Hairfoot,
Oh so long ago.
Oh you know it was taken by the Hairfoot,
Oh so long ago.
Oh Lord don't hold me back now
'Cause I ain't to far for to go
First ole Bilbo he stole my ring,
Then he tooks it to Shire.
And now little Frodo's got it,
He's gonna throw it in the fire.
Oh Lord I'm goin',
Goin' down to Mordor town.
And ifn I can't gets my ring back,
Lord it's time to lay me down.

I hope by now you can see how music from this targeted group can be traced directly to the slave quarters and fields, especially the Blues and Negro Spirituals.

tt

EVENT NUMBER 11

GRAVEYARDS OR CEMETERIES

EVENT: There was a time in America, especially in the south, when all members of the targeted group were buried in Graveyards, not Cemeteries. In fact, the word Cemetery is a European word and those who are buried in them usually are of European descent. Graveyards that have been standing long before slavery ended in 1865, are now changing to Cemeteries. I don't think many have a clue as to the difference between the two. Graveyards have a way of telling who you are and where you came from. This we should not give up

BEHAVIOR: The people of Africa and Asia used Graveyards to bury their dead. You can go back into antiquity and you will find the same. When Israel died in Egypt land, his son Joseph was at his bedside. Israel told Joseph where he wished to be buried, back in Canaan. In the scripture below, Joseph is sending word to the king of Egypt as to what his father's last request was: To be buried in the GRAVE he dug before he left.

"My father made me swear, saying, "Behold, I am dying; in my grave which I dug for myself in the land of Canaan, there you shall bury me." Now therefore, please let me go up and bury my father, and I will come back" {Genesis 50:5}

Even during Jesus' time, people were buried in graves. When Lazarus died his sisters, Mary and Martha sent for Jesus. By the time Jesus arrived Lazarus had been dead for four days. In fact, the bible tells us he was already smelling. That was the condition Jesus found him in. It is recorded in the Bible that Lazarus was buried in a GRAVE.

John 12:17

The people therefore that was with him when he called Lazarus out of his grave, and raised him from the dead, bare record.

If for no other reason, the name GRAVEYARD should remain to denote who was buried there. I am not advocating when a member of the targeted group dies the body should be deposited in a Graveyard. I am saying where there are long standing GRAVEYARDS whose people have been deposited on that site for over a hundred years, using the name GRAVEYARD, there should not be a reason compelling enough to change the word from GRAVEYARD to Cemetery.

Information below will shed some light on the origin of cemeteries.

THE COLUMBIA ENCYCLOPEDIA, SIX EDITION, 2001

"The name *cemetery* was used by early Christians to designate a place for burying the dead. First applied in Christian burials in the Roman catacombs, the word *cemetery* came into general usage in the 15th cent. Group burials have been found in Paleolithis caves and fields of prehistoric grave mounds, or barrows, are located throughout Europe, Asia, and North America. In the ancient Middle East, graves were often grouped around temples and sanctuaries. In Greece the dead were buried outside the city walls along the roads leading into the city in a necropolis (city of the dead). Christians belief in resurrection made chapel crypts and churchyards desirable for burial, but overcrowding and the rise of urbans centers made it necessary to establish cemetery plots outside the city limits. Graveyards of all periods tend to reflect the familial and class groupings of their living society. Among the many beautiful and historic cemeteries of Europe are the Pere-Lachaise in Paris and the Campo Santo in Pisa. A noteworthy U.S cemetery is the Arlington National Cemetary. The National Park Service also maintains cemeteries (see National Parks and Monuments table). See funeral customs; grave, tomb".

Some have associated ghost with Cemeteries and haunts

(HANTS) with Graveyards. Ghosts are usually viewed as friendly. Casper the Ghost is a friendly one. On the other hand, most of my childhood, I have heard of headless haunted horses. These Haunts, as the story was told, came up out of the Graves to instill fear into the hearts to those subjects that came in contact with them. The Graveyard was always viewed as a haunted place where the haunts usually come out at night. Old men were fearful of haunts in the community I was raised.

During the Civil War, rich men in the south buried their strongest slaves with their money so that if anyone tried to dig the money up, these buried slaves would rise up from the grave to haunt those digging where the money was buried, so the story goes. That story was believed where I was raised. Many men carried whiskey around with them at night. Word had it that the Hants (HANTS) loved whiskey and would get off your trail if you sprinkled some on the ground. I heard some men say it worked for them. Others were said to be born with a veil over their face so that they can see Haunts in the dark.

In most southern cities Anglo American Cemeteries are located near or in the African American community. You will be hard pressed to find a Cemetery in the white community, especially in small cities. Several explanations have been offered for this fact. First, whites are afraid of their dead. Next, they bury their people among African Americans to keep them in the community when night comes, knowing their beliefs on Haunts and Ghosts. Whatever the reason for selecting African American communities for a burying site, check and you will see exactly where Cemeteries are located in the south.

Endnotes

[12] Life and Times of Frederick Douglass, by himself, Collier Books, New York , New York (1892) p.353.